·*Cooking for Today*·

CLASSIC INDIAN COOKING

·Cooking for Today·

CLASSIC INDIAN COOKING

CARA HOBDAY

A Siena Book
Siena is an imprint of Parragon Books

First published in Great Britain in 1996 by
Parragon Book Service Ltd
Unit 13–17
Avonbridge Trading Estate
Atlantic Road
Avonmouth
Bristol BS11 9QD

ISBN 0-7525-1530-6

Produced by Haldane Mason, London

Printed in Italy

Acknowledgements:
Art Direction: Ron Samuels
Editor: Michael Williams
Series Design: Pedro & Frances Prá-Lopez/Kingfisher Design
Page Design: Somewhere Creative
Photography: Iain Bagwell
Styling: Rachel Jukes
Home Economist: Cara Hobday

Photographs on pages 6, 20, 34, 48 and 62 are reproduced by permission of
ZEFA Picture Library (UK) Ltd

Note:
Cup measurements in this book are for American cups. Tablespoons are assumed to be 15 ml.
Unless otherwise stated, milk is assumed to be full-fat, eggs are standard size 3, butter is unsalted (sweet), and
pepper is freshly ground black pepper.

Contents

CHAPTER ONE

Mild Dishes

Milder dishes are a speciality of northern India, where richer flavours are enjoyed and dairy products are more prevalent. These recipes have a delicate balance of flavours and spice mixes, and extra chilli should not be added to heat them up.

The sauces in this chapter are the kind that the delicate palates of the maharajahs and nazirs of a long ago India might have had prepared for their delectation. Indian cooking can be divided into two definite sections – dishes that are eaten by the ordinary people, prepared by simple methods from basic ingredients, and dishes that are eaten by the upper ranks of society, which are full of subtle spice mixes and sophisticated methods. Kitchens of the wealthy employ a brigade of skilled chefs, one of whom, the *masalchi*, spice grinder, is responsible for the spices. He gathers together all the spices that the chefs will need for the day and grinds them by hand using a pestle and mortar, either individually or mixed together in varying proportions for different mixes and dishes. When all the mixes are right and all the required seeds ground, the spice grinder passes them on to the chefs, who will use skill to get the full flavour out of each spice, adding each one to the dish at the right moment, to achieve a good balance and harmony in the dish.

Opposite: *The Taj Mahal – the essence of India.*

STEP 1

STEP 2

STEP 3

STEP 4

SAFFRON CHICKEN

This is a beautifully aromatic dish, the full fragrance of which brings to mind the opulent days of the maharajahs, with their desert fortresses, lake-side palaces and water gardens.

SERVES 4

*large pinch of saffron strands, about 30
    strands
50 ml/2 fl oz/4 tbsp boiling water
4 chicken supremes
3 tbsp ghee
1/2 tsp coriander seeds, ground
1 dried bay leaf
2.5 cm/1 inch piece cinnamon stick
30 g/1 oz/1 1/2 tbsp sultanas (golden raisins)
300 ml/1/2 pint/1 1/4 cups natural yogurt
15 g/1/2 oz/2 tbsp flaked (slivered) almonds,
    toasted
salt and pepper*

1 Combine the saffron with the boiling water, and leave to steep for 10 minutes.

2 Season the chicken pieces well.

3 Heat the ghee in a large frying pan (skillet), add the chicken pieces and brown on both sides. Cook in batches if necessary. Remove the chicken from the pan.

4 Reduce the heat to medium and add the coriander to the pan, stir once and add the bay leaf, cinnamon

stick, sultanas (golden raisins) and the saffron with the soaking water all at once.

5 Return the chicken to the pan. Cover and simmer gently for 40–50 minutes or until the chicken juices run clear when the thickest part of each piece is pierced with a sharp knife. Remove the pan from the heat and gently stir the yogurt into the sauce.

6 Discard the bay leaf and cinnamon stick. Scatter over the toasted almonds and serve.

CHICKEN

The chicken supreme is the breast on the bone, with part of the wing bone still attached; it does not dry out as much as the breast fillet during long cooking, and, in my opinion, has more flavour. Chicken supremes are available from butchers and most supermarkets.

STEP 1

STEP 3

STEP 4

STEP 5

SHAHI MURG

Shahi Murg is a traditional curry cooked in yogurt by a method that is used to make a lot of the sauces in India. They are thickened by long cooking, which separates the yogurt and evaporates the water content. The resulting dishes are delicious, but do take perseverance to make!

SERVES 4

1 tsp cumin seeds
1 tsp coriander seeds
2 tbsp ghee
1 onion, sliced finely
8 small–medium chicken pieces
1/2 tsp salt
350 ml/ 12 fl oz/ 1 1/2 cups natural yogurt
120 ml/ 4 fl oz/ 1/2 cup double cream
1 tbsp ground almonds
1/2 tsp Garam Masala (see page 76)
3 cloves
seeds from 3 green cardamom pods
1 dried bay leaf
60 g/ 2 oz/ 1/3 cup sultanas (golden raisins)
fresh coriander (cilantro) sprigs to garnish

1 Grind together the cumin and coriander seeds in a spice grinder or a pestle and mortar.

2 Heat half the ghee in a large saucepan and cook the onion over a medium heat for 15 minutes, stirring occasionally, until the onion is very soft and sweet.

3 Meanwhile, heat the remaining ghee in a large frying pan (skillet) and brown the chicken pieces well. Add to the onions.

4 Add the ground cumin, ground coriander, salt, yogurt, cream, almonds and garam masala.

5 Bring to a gentle simmer, and add the cloves, cardamom, bay leaf and sultanas (golden raisins).

6 Simmer for 40 minutes until the chicken juices run clear when the thickest part of each piece is pierced with a sharp knife, and the sauce has reduced and thickened.

7 Serve garnished with coriander (cilantro) sprigs.

HANDY HINT

The cloves and bay leaf are not meant to be eaten. I find that it is easier to put them to one side of the plate than to discard them before serving; I never have time to fish about for hours looking for three cloves in a pot of curry, while hungry mouths are waiting!

STEP 1

STEP 2

STEP 3

STEP 6

RASHMI KEBABS

This is a variation on Sheek Kebab (see page 30). A little attention is needed when making the egg 'nets', but the extra effort is worth it, as the effect is very impressive.

SERVES 4

1 red (bell) pepper, deseeded and chopped
   coarsely
1 tsp chilli powder
2 tsp coriander seeds
2 tsp cumin seeds
$1/2$ tsp salt
2 cloves garlic
$1/2$ tsp ground black pepper
500 g/1 lb/2 cups minced (ground) lamb
4 eggs
oil for deep frying

1 Grind the red (bell) pepper, chilli powder, coriander seeds, cumin seeds, salt, garlic and black pepper in a food processor or blender. Alternatively, grind the coriander and cumin in a pestle and mortar, chop the red (bell) pepper and garlic very finely and mix with the ground spices, salt, chilli powder and black pepper.

2 Transfer the spice mixture to a bowl and add the lamb and 1 of the eggs. Mix well to evenly distribute the egg and bind the mixture together.

3 Divide the lamb mixture into 8. Shape 1 piece into a ball. Put the ball on a clean plate and gently squash

the top with the palm of your hand, to form a patty. Repeat with the remaining pieces. If possible, refrigerate the kebabs for at least 30 minutes.

4 Cook the kebabs under a preheated hot grill (broiler) for 15 minutes, turning once.

5 Meanwhile, make the egg nets. Beat together the remaining eggs. Fill a large frying pan (skillet) with oil to a depth of 5–7.5 cm/2–3 inches. Heat until a cube of bread that is dropped in sizzles in 1 minute.

6 Trickle the egg off the end of a spoon into the oil, crisscrossing the lines in a grid shape. It will take only seconds to cook. Remove and drain on plenty of paper towels. Repeat until all the egg is used. Wrap each kebab in 1–2 egg nets. Serve warm.

HANDY HINT

Refrigerating the kebabs for at least 30 minutes sets them and ensures that they keep their shape when cooked.

CHICKEN JALFREZI

This is a quick and tasty way to use leftover roast chicken. The sauce can also be used for any cooked poultry, lamb or beef. For extra crunch, add whatever vegetables you have to hand.

STEP 1

SERVES 4

1 tsp mustard oil
3 tbsp vegetable oil
1 large onion, chopped finely
3 garlic cloves, crushed
1 tbsp tomato purée (paste)
2 tomatoes, peeled and chopped
1 tsp ground turmeric
$\frac{1}{2}$ tsp cumin seeds, ground
$\frac{1}{2}$ tsp coriander seeds, ground
$\frac{1}{2}$ tsp chilli powder
$\frac{1}{2}$ tsp Garam Masala (see page 76)
1 tsp red wine vinegar
1 small red (bell) pepper, chopped
125 g/4 oz/1 cup frozen broad (fava) beans
500 g/1 lb cooked chicken, cut into bite-
   sized pieces
$\frac{1}{2}$ tsp salt
fresh coriander (cilantro) sprigs to garnish

1 Heat the mustard oil in a large, frying pan (skillet) set over a high heat for about 1 minute until it begins to smoke. Add the vegetable oil, reduce the heat and then add the onion and the garlic. Fry oil, garlic and onion until they are golden.

2 Add the tomato purée (paste), chopped tomatoes, turmeric, ground cumin, ground coriander, chilli

STEP 2

powder, garam masala and vinegar to the frying pan (skillet). Stir the mixture until fragrant.

3 Add the red (bell) pepper and broad (fava) beans and stir for 2 minutes until the pepper is softened.

4 Stir in the chicken, and salt to taste. Simmer gently for 6–8 minutes until the chicken is heated through and the beans are tender.

5 Serve garnished with coriander (cilantro) sprigs.

STEP 2

USING LEFTOVERS

This dish is an ideal way of making use of leftover poultry – turkey, duck or quail. Any variety of bean works well, but vegetables are just as useful, especially root vegetables, courgettes, potatoes or broccoli. Leafy vegetables will not be so successful.

STEP 3

STEP 1

STEP 2

STEP 3

STEP 5

LAMB BIRIANI

In India this elaborate, beautifully coloured dish is usually served at parties and on festive occasions. This version can be made on any day, festive or not.

SERVES 4

250 g/8 oz/generous 1 cup basmati rice,
   washed and drained
1/2 tsp salt
2 garlic cloves, peeled and left whole
2.5 cm/1 inch piece ginger root, grated
4 cloves
1/2 tsp black peppercorns
2 green cardamom pods
1 tsp cumin seeds
1 tsp coriander seeds
2.5 cm/1 inch piece cinnamon stick
1 tsp saffron strands
50 ml/2 fl oz/4 tbsp tepid water
2 tbsp ghee
2 shallots, sliced
1/4 tsp grated nutmeg
1/4 tsp chilli powder
500 g/1 lb boneless leg of lamb, cut into
   2.5 cm/1 inch cubes
180 ml/6 fl oz/3/4 cup natural yogurt
30 g/1 oz/ 2 tbsp sultanas (golden raisins)
30 g /1 oz/1/4 cup flaked (slivered) almonds,
   toasted

1 Bring a large saucepan of salted water to the boil. Add the rice and boil for 6 minutes. Drain and set aside.

2 Grind together the garlic, ginger, cloves, peppercorns, cardamom pods, cumin, coriander and cinnamon.

3 Combine saffron and water, and set aside. Heat the ghee in a large saucepan and add shallots. Fry until golden brown then add the ground spice mix, nutmeg and chilli powder. Stir for 1 minute and add the lamb. Cook until evenly browned.

4 Add the yogurt, stirring constantly, then the sultanas (golden raisins) and bring to a simmer. Cook for 40 minutes, stirring occasionally.

5 Carefully pile the rice on the sauce, in a pyramid shape. Trickle the saffron and soaking water over the rice in lines. Cover the pan with a clean tea towel or dish towel and put the lid on. Reduce the heat to low and cook for 10 minutes. Remove the lid and tea towel, and quickly make 3 holes in the rice with a wooden spoon handle, to the level of the sauce, but not touching it. Replace the tea towel and the lid and leave to stand for 5 minutes.

6 Remove the lid and tea towel, lightly fork the rice and serve, sprinkled with the toasted almonds.

STEP 1

STEP 2

STEP 4

STEP 5

STUFFED PARATHAS

To make parathas successfully, be sure to knead the dough until it is quite smooth and to roll it out as thinly as you can.

SERVES 4–8

250 g/8 oz/2 cups wholemeal
  (wholewheat) flour
250 g/8 oz/2 cups plain (all-purpose) flour
120–180 ml/4–6 fl oz/½–¾ cup water
1 tbsp ghee
1 onion, chopped
2.5 cm/1 inch piece cinnamon stick
1 dried bay leaf
1 dried red chilli
¼ tsp ground turmeric
1 tsp coriander seeds, ground
1 tsp cumin seeds, ground
500 g/1 lb/2 cups lean minced (ground)
  beef
150 ml/¼ pint/⅔ cup natural yogurt
125 g/4 oz/¾ cup frozen peas
60 g/2 oz/¼ cup butter, melted
salt and pepper
chopped fresh coriander (cilantro) to garnish

1 Sift the two flours and a pinch of salt together into a bowl and make a well in the centre.

2 Gradually add water to make a soft dough, and knead until smooth and no longer sticky. Set aside.

3 Heat the ghee in a large frying pan (skillet) and fry the onion until golden brown. Stir in the cinnamon, bay leaf, chilli, turmeric, ground coriander, cumin and minced (ground) beef for 1 minute. Add the yogurt and cook over a high heat until the beef is dry. Add the peas, season to taste and simmer for 8–10 minutes.

4 To make the parathas, divide the dough into 6 or 8 pieces. Roll each piece into a ball, then roll out to a 25 cm/ 10 inch round.

5 Brush the upper side with melted butter. Fold in half, and spoon 1 tablespoon of the stuffing into the centre of each folded piece. Fold each half in half again so that you are left with cone shapes.

6 Gently heat a large frying pan (skillet) and place a paratha in it. Brush each side lightly with a little melted butter and cook over a medium heat for 3–4 minutes. Do not let the pan get too hot. Turn over and cook the other side for 3–4 minutes. Keep warm and repeat with the remaining parathas. Serve immediately.

CHAPTER TWO

Medium Dishes

The dishes in this chapter are ideal for serving with a selection of pickles and breads at dinner.

There are as many variations on each dish as there are cooks, because each cook has his or her favourite spice mix and method of cooking to produce a flavour that is unique. So you can imagine the variation in Indian cookbooks, each one proudly claiming that its recipes are the best, just as every Indian restaurant proclaims its recipe to be the most original. Although some purists may protest, 'but this is not the *real* cuisine of India', it is what we in the West have come to see as Indian, and unless we are lucky enough to take the few thousand-mile round trip to India, we are unlikely to experience anything different. Therefore, I have included some dishes that you will recognize and may even be familiar with from Indian restaurant menus. These are my recipes, so they may not taste precisely the same as your local curry house, but the key elements are the same. Unlike mild dishes, the heat in these recipes can be varied by increasing or reducing the chilli content.

Opposite: *Mount Annapurna provides a magnificent backdrop for a traditional house in Nepal.*

LAMB DO PYAZA

Do Pyaza usually indicates a dish of meat cooked with plenty of onions. In this recipe the onions are cooked in two different ways: half are fried at the beginning, and the other half are added later to give a more pungent, fresher onion flavour.

STEP 1

SERVES 4

2 tbsp ghee
2 large onions, sliced finely
4 garlic cloves, 2 of them crushed
750 g/ 1¹/₂ lb boneless lamb shoulder, cut
    into 2.5 cm/ 1 inch cubes
1 tsp chilli powder
2.5 cm/ 1 inch piece ginger root, grated
2 fresh green chillies, chopped
¹/₂ tsp ground turmeric
¹/₂ tsp salt and ground black pepper
180 ml/ 6 fl oz/ ³/₄ cup natural yogurt
2 cloves
2.5 cm/ 1 inch piece cinnamon stick
300 ml/ ¹/₂ pint/ 1¹/₄ cups water
2 tbsp chopped fresh coriander (cilantro)
3 tbsp lemon juice
naan bread to serve

1 Heat the ghee in a large saucepan and add 1 of the onions and the garlic. Cook for 2–3 minutes, stirring constantly.

2 Add the lamb and brown all over. Remove and set aside.

3 Add the chilli powder, ginger, chillies and turmeric and stir for a further 30 seconds.

4 Add plenty of salt and pepper, the yogurt, cloves, cinnamon and water. Return the lamb to the pan. Bring to the boil then simmer for 10 minutes.

5 Transfer to an ovenproof dish and place uncovered in a preheated oven at 180°C/350°F/Gas mark 4 for 40 minutes. Check the seasoning.

6 Stir in the remaining onion and cook uncovered for a further 40 minutes.

7 Add the fresh coriander (cilantro) and lemon juice. Serve with naan bread.

STEP 3

STEP 4

ADVANCE PREPARATION

This curry definitely improves if made in advance and then reheated before serving. This develops the flavours and makes them deeper. The dish will also freeze successfully for up to 6 weeks.

STEP 6

STEP 1

STEP 2

STEP 3

STEP 4

KARAHI CHICKEN

A Karahi is a two-handled metal pan that is similar to a wok. Food is always cooked over a high heat in a karahi. It's an extremely versatile piece of equipment.

SERVES 4–6

2 tbsp ghee
3 garlic cloves, crushed
1 onion, chopped finely
2 tbsp Garam Masala (see page 76)
1 tsp coriander seeds, ground
$\frac{1}{2}$ tsp dried mint
1 dried bay leaf
750 g/1$\frac{1}{2}$ lb boneless chicken meat, diced
200 ml/7 fl oz/scant 1 cup chicken stock or
    water
1 tbsp finely chopped fresh coriander
    (cilantro)
salt
naan bread or chapatis to serve

1 Heat the ghee in a karahi or wok, or a large, heavy frying pan (skillet) and add the garlic and onion. Stir for about 4 minutes until the onion is golden.

2 Stir in the garam masala, ground coriander, mint and bay leaf.

3 Add the chicken and cook over a high heat, stirring occasionally, for about 5 minutes.

4 Add the stock or water and simmer for 10 minutes, until the sauce has thickened and the chicken juices run clear when the meat is tested with a sharp knife.

5 Stir in the fresh coriander (cilantro), salt to taste and serve immediately with naan bread or chapatis.

SERVING
SUGGESTIONS

Take the sizzling curry to the table in the pan on which it was cooked, and serve a huge pile of naan bread or chapatis for scooping up the curry from the dish.

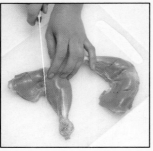

STEP 1

STEP 2

STEP 3

STEP 4

TANDOORI CHICKEN

The traditional Indian tandoor oven is a huge urn. Charcoal is burnt slowly at the bottom of the oven until it becomes a mass of white hot coals. It is then ready for cooking food at a very high temperature. To replicate this in a Western kitchen, cook the tandoori chicken at a very high temperature, preferably on a barbecue.

SERVES 4

8 small chicken portions, skinned
3 dried red chillies
1 tsp salt
2 tsp coriander seeds
2 tbsp lime juice
2 garlic cloves, crushed
2.5 cm/1 inch piece ginger root, grated
1 clove
2 tsp Garam Masala (see page 76)
2 tsp chilli powder
1/2 onion, chopped and rinsed
300 ml/1/2 pint/1 1/4 cups natural yogurt
1 tbsp chopped fresh coriander (cilantro)
lemon slices to garnish
Cucumber Raita (see below) to serve

1 Make 2–3 slashes with a sharp knife in the flesh of the chicken pieces.

2 Crush together the chillies, salt, coriander seeds, lime juice, garlic, ginger and clove. Stir in the garam masala and chilli powder. Transfer to a small saucepan and heat gently until aromatic.

3 Add the onion and fry. Then stir in yogurt and remove pan from heat.

4 Arrange the chicken in a non-metallic dish and pour over the yogurt mixture. Cover and put in the refrigerator to marinate for 4 hours or overnight.

5 Arrange the chicken on a grill (broiler) tray and cook under a preheated very hot grill (broiler) or over a barbecue for 20–30 minutes, turning once, until the chicken juices run clear when the thickest parts of the portions are pierced with a sharp knife.

6 Sprinkle the chicken with chopped fresh coriander (cilantro). Serve hot or cold, garnished with the lemon slices and accompanied by cucumber raita.

CUCUMBER RAITA

Mix together 250 g/8 oz/1 cup natural yogurt, 2 tsp chopped fresh mint, 175 g/6 oz cucumber, peeled, deseeded and cut into matchsticks, and salt to taste. Serve as a cooling accompaniment to any spicy dish.

LAMB PASANDA

This dish is as close as one gets to the classic curry that springs to mind when Indian Cooking is mentioned.

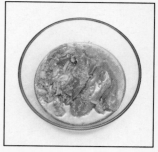

STEP 2

SERVES 4

500 g/1 lb boneless lamb shoulder
150 ml/¼ pint/⅔ cup red wine
75 ml/3 fl oz/⅓ cup oil
3 garlic cloves, crushed
5 cm/2 inch piece ginger root, grated
1 tsp coriander seeds, ground
1 tsp cumin seeds, ground
2 tbsp ghee
1 large onion, chopped
1 tsp Garam Masala (see page 76)
2 fresh green chillies, halved
300 ml/½ pint/1¼ cups natural yogurt
2 tbsp ground almonds
20 whole blanched almonds
salt

1 Cut the lamb into strips 2.5 cm/1 inch across and 10 cm/4 inches long. Set aside.

2 Combine the red wine, oil, garlic, ginger, coriander and cumin in a large non-metallic bowl. Stir in the lamb and leave to marinate for 1 hour.

3 Heat the ghee in a frying pan (skillet) and fry the onion until brown.

4 Drain the lamb, reserving the contents of the bowl. Pat the lamb dry with paper towels. Add the lamb to the frying pan (skillet) and stir over a high heat until it is evenly sealed and browned.

5 Add the contents of the bowl to the pan, and bring to a gentle boil. Add the garam masala, chillies, yogurt, ground almonds, whole almonds, and salt to taste. Cover and simmer for 12–15 minutes until the lamb is tender.

STEP 3

MUTTON

In India mutton is often used for curries; it has a lovely full flavour and stands up well to the long cooking of most curries. It is well worth searching for. If you would like to use it for this recipe, marinate boneless shoulder, uncovered, in the refrigerator for 4–5 hours or overnight. Simmer for 1 hour, skimming the surface as necessary to remove any fat, before adding the garam masala, chillies, yogurt and almonds.

STEP 4

STEP 5

STEP 1

STEP 2

STEP 3

STEP 4

SHEEK KEBABS

Sheek Kebabs are delicious cooked over a barbecue. Serve in pitta bread for great party food. The cooked meat can also be chopped into a salad.

SERVES 4–8

1 tsp coriander seeds
1 tsp cumin seeds
1 clove
2.5 cm/1 inch piece ginger root, chopped
1 tsp ground turmeric
1 fresh red chilli, deseeded and chopped
1/2 tsp ground cinnamon
1 tsp ground black pepper
1/2 tsp salt
125 g/4 oz/1/2 cup minced (ground) beef
350 g/12 oz/11/2 cups minced (ground)
   lamb
1 onion, chopped finely
1 egg

TO SERVE:
salad
Cucumber Raita (see page 26)

1 Grind together the coriander, cumin, clove and ginger in a pestle and mortar. Mix in the turmeric, chilli, cinnamon, pepper and salt.

2 Combine the spice mixture with the beef, lamb and onion.

3 Make a well in the centre of the meat mixture, add the egg and mix in thoroughly.

4 Press one-eighth of the meat mixture around an oiled skewer, to form a shape about 10 cm/4 inches long and 2.5 cm/1 inch thick. Repeat with the remaining meat mixture.

5 If possible, leave to rest in the refrigerator for at least 1 hour.

6 Cook the kebabs under a preheated medium grill (broiler) for about 20 minutes, turning once or twice, until the meat juices run clear when the thickest part of the meat balls is pierced with the point of a sharp knife.

7 Serve with salad and cucumber raita.

WOODEN SKEWERS

Wooden skewers should be soaked in hot water for 20 minutes before they are used, to prevent them from burning.

STEP 2

STEP 4

STEP 6

STEP 7

ROGAN JOSH

Rogan Josh is one of the best-known curries and is a great favourite in restaurants. The title means 'red curry', the red being provided by the chillies.

SERVES 6

2 tbsp ghee
1 kg/2 lb braising steak, cut into 2.5 cm/
*   1 inch cubes*
1 onion, chopped finely
3 garlic cloves
2.5 cm/1 inch piece ginger root, grated
4 fresh red chillies, chopped
4 green cardamom pods
4 cloves
2 tsp coriander seeds
2 tsp cumin seeds
1 tsp paprika
1 tsp salt
1 dried bay leaf
120 ml/4 fl oz/$\frac{1}{2}$ cup natural yogurt
2.5 cm/1 inch piece cinnamon stick
150 ml/$\frac{1}{4}$ pint/$\frac{2}{3}$ cups hot water
$\frac{1}{4}$ tsp Garam Masala (see page 76)
pepper

1 Heat the ghee in a large flameproof casserole and brown the meat in batches. Set aside in a bowl.

2 Add the onion to the ghee and stir over a high heat for 3–4 minutes.

3 Grind together the garlic, ginger, chillies, cardamom, cloves, coriander, cumin, paprika and salt.

4 Add the spice paste and bay leaf to the casserole and stir until fragrant.

5 Return the meat and any juices in the bowl to the casserole and simmer for 2–3 minutes.

6 Gradually stir the yogurt into the casserole so that the sauce keeps simmering.

7 Stir in the cinnamon and hot water, and pepper to taste.

8 Cover and cook in a preheated oven at 180°C/350°F/Gas mark 4 for 1¼ hours, stirring frequently, until the meat is very tender and the sauce is slightly reduced.

9 Discard the cinnamon stick and stir in the garam masala. Remove surplus oil from the surface of the casserole before serving.

CHAPTER THREE

Fiery Dishes

These recipes are for more experienced curry eaters. The spice mixes in these dishes take as much balancing and harmonizing as in the mild dishes where the only flavours are the spices. In these hotter dishes, the spices have to provide a deeper flavour, such as the sweetness in Lamb Bhuna (see page 36) or the sharpness in Vindaloo Curry (see page 44).

If you are serving a selection of dishes for an Indian-style dinner, include a fiery curry for those who feel that the other dishes are too mild and to provide the more timid guests with a wider experience. Be sure to offer plenty of rice, bread, raitas and vegetable dishes to accompany a hot curry. These are more effective at diluting the heat than water, and allow the fuller flavours to be appreciated. In fact, drinking water is the wrong thing to do. However, in my experience, if somebody selects a fiery curry by mistake, while their tongue is on fire and their eyes are on stalks, the last thing they want to hear is 'Just eat some rice, and you will be fine'; they would rather be passed the water jug – no glass, just the whole jug!

The flavours and heat in a fiery dish smooth out if it is made in advance then reheated when required.

Opposite: The teeming riverside at Varanasi on the River Ganges.

STEP 1

STEP 3

STEP 4

STEP 5

LAMB BHUNA

The pungent flavours of the chillies in this curry should not hide the flavours of the other spices. However, you do have to become accustomed to the strong chillies before these subtle flavours can be appreciated!

SERVES 4–6

1 onion, chopped
2 garlic cloves
3 tomatoes, peeled and chopped
1 tsp malt vinegar
1 tbsp oil
750 g/1½ lb lean boneless lamb, cut into
    4 cm/1½ inch cubes
2 tsp coriander seeds, ground
1 tsp cumin seeds, ground
2 dried red chillies, chopped
3 fresh green chillies, chopped
½ tsp ground turmeric
30 g/1 oz/2 tbsp creamed coconut
50 ml/2 fl oz/4 tbsp water
1 tsp Garam Masala (see page 76)
salt and pepper
fresh coriander (cilantro) leaves to garnish

1 Purée the onion, garlic, tomatoes and vinegar in a food processor or blender. Alternatively, chop the vegetables finely by hand, then mix with the vinegar. Set aside.

2 Heat the oil in a large frying pan (skillet) and brown the meat for 5–10 minutes. Remove and set aside.

3 Reduce the heat beneath the pan and add the ground coriander

seeds, cumin, chillies and turmeric. Stir continuously until the spices are fragrant.

4 Increase the heat again and add the onion mixture. Stir-fry for 5 minutes until nearly dry.

5 Return the meat to the pan. Combine the coconut and water and add to the pan. Simmer for 45–60 minutes until the meat is tender. Stir in the garam masala and season to taste.

6 Serve garnished with fresh coriander (cilantro) leaves.

CREAMED COCONUT

Creamed coconut can be bought in block form and is extremely convenient to keep on hand. Coconut milk can be made by dissolving creamed coconut in an equal quantity of tepid water. The addition of creamed coconut or coconut milk adds richness to a dish and, if used in small quantities gives a good depth of flavour.

LAMB TIKKA MASALA

This is a very rich dish, and is best enjoyed with simple accompaniments, such as dal (see pages 64 and 66), naan bread, a salad and some plain basmati rice.

STEP 1

SERVES 6

1 tsp cumin seeds, ground
$^1/_2$ tsp ground turmeric
5 cm/2 inch piece ginger root, grated
2 garlic cloves, crushed
$^1/_2$ tsp salt
120 ml/4 fl oz/$^1/_2$ cup natural yogurt
1 kg/2 lb boneless lamb, cut into 2.5 cm/
    1 inch cubes
1–2 drops edible red food colouring
1 tsp water
fresh mint leaves to garnish

MASALA SAUCE:
1 tbsp ghee
3 tomatoes, peeled and chopped
$^1/_2$ tsp yellow mustard seed
2 fresh green chillies, chopped
120 ml/4 fl oz/$^1/_2$ cup coconut milk
3 tbsp chopped fresh mint
3 tbsp chopped fresh coriander (cilantro)
salt

1 Combine the cumin, turmeric, ginger, garlic, salt and yogurt in a bowl. Stir in the lamb until evenly coated with the sauce. Dilute the food colouring with the water, and add to the bowl, stirring well. Marinate in the refrigerator for 2 hours. Soak 6 wooden skewers in warm water for 15 minutes.

2 Make the masala sauce. Heat the ghee in a large saucepan and add the tomatoes, mustard seeds, green chillies and coconut milk. Bring to the boil, then simmer for 20 minutes until the tomatoes have broken down. Stir occasionally.

3 Thread the pieces of lamb on to 6 oiled skewers. Set on a grill (broiler) pan and cook under a preheated very hot grill for 15–20 minutes, turning occasionally.

4 Stir the mint and fresh coriander (cilantro) into the sauce, and season with salt.

5 Carefully remove the lamb from the skewers. Stir the lamb into the sauce and serve garnished with mint leaves.

STEP 2

MARINATING

Marinating can be reduced to 1 hour by piercing each piece of meat thoroughly with a skewer. Warm the marinade so that none of the liquid evaporates and the flavours do not change, then pour it over the meat, rubbing it in well.

STEP 3

STEP 5

CHICKEN TIKKA MASALA

Serve this very rich dish with an array of accompaniments to provide a balance and to neutralize the fiery flavours. Try serving the chicken with mango chutney, lime pickle and Cucumber Raita (see page 26). Add poppadoms and basmati rice to make a delicious meal.

STEP 1

SERVES 4

½ onion, chopped coarsely
60 g/2 oz/3 tbsp tomato purée (paste)
1 tsp cumin seeds
2.5 cm/1 inch piece ginger root, chopped
3 tbsp lemon juice
2 garlic cloves, crushed
2 tsp chilli powder
750 g/1½ lb boneless chicken
salt and pepper
fresh mint sprigs to garnish

MASALA SAUCE:
2 tbsp ghee
1 onion, sliced
1 tbsp black onion seeds
3 garlic cloves, crushed
2 fresh green chillies, chopped
200 g/7 oz can tomatoes
120 ml/4 fl oz/½ cup natural yogurt
120 ml/4 fl oz/½ cup coconut milk
1 tbsp chopped fresh coriander (cilantro)
1 tbsp chopped fresh mint
2 tbsp lemon or lime juice
½ tsp Garam Masala (see page 76)

1 Combine the onion, tomato purée (paste), cumin, ginger, lemon juice, garlic, chilli powder and salt and pepper in a food processor or blender and then transfer to a bowl. Alternatively, grind the cumin in a pestle and mortar and transfer to a bowl. Finely chop the onion and ginger and stir into the bowl with the tomato purée (paste), lemon juice, salt and pepper, garlic and chilli powder.

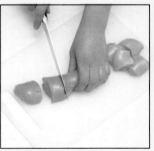

STEP 2

2 Cut chicken into 4 cm/1½ inch cubes. Stir into the bowl and leave to marinate for 2 hours.

3 Make the masala sauce. Heat the ghee in a large saucepan, add the onion and stir over a medium heat for 5 minutes. Add the onion seeds, garlic and chillies and cook until fragrant.

STEP 3

4 Add the tomatoes, yogurt and coconut milk, bring to the boil, then simmer for 20 minutes.

5 Meanwhile, divide the chicken evenly between 8 oiled skewers and cook under a preheated very hot grill (broiler) for 15 minutes, turning frequently. Remove the chicken from the skewers and add to the sauce. Stir in the fresh coriander (cilantro), mint, lemon or lime juice, and garam masala. Serve garnished with mint sprigs.

STEP 4

STEP 2

STEP 3

STEP 4

STEP 4

LAMB PHALL

Many a time this dish has been chosen in an Indian restaurant by customers who soon live to regret it – usually after the fifth jug of water! For those more used to hot curries this is a delicious dish. Do try to use freshly ground whole spices, as they will make the overall taste more complex and enjoyable.

SERVES 4–6

8 fresh or dried red chillies, or to taste
4 tbsp ghee
1 onion, chopped finely
6 garlic cloves, chopped finely
5 cm/2 inch piece ginger root, chopped finely
1 tsp cumin seeds, ground
1 tsp coriander seeds, ground
1 tsp fenugreek seeds, ground
1 tsp Garam Masala (see page 76)
425 g/14 oz can tomatoes
1 tbsp tomato ketchup
1 tbsp tomato purée (paste)
750 g/1½ lb boneless lamb shoulder, cut
  into 5 cm/2 inch cubes

TO SERVE:
Cucumber Raita (see page 26)
pickles

1 Chop 4 of the chillies and leave the other 4 whole.

2 Heat half of the ghee in a saucepan and add the onion, garlic and ginger. Stir over a medium heat until golden.

3 Stir the cumin, coriander, fenugreek and garam masala into the onion. Cook over a medium heat for 10 minutes.

4 Stir the canned tomatoes, tomato ketchup, tomato purée (paste) and the whole and chopped chillies into the pan, and bring to a gentle boil. Cook over a low heat for 10 minutes.

5 Meanwhile, heat the remaining ghee in a flameproof casserole and cook the meat until evenly sealed. Cook in batches if necessary.

6 Transfer the sauce to the casserole with the meat, cover and cook in a preheated oven at 180°C/350°F/Gas mark 4 for 1½ hours until the meat is tender.

7 Serve with cucumber raita and pickles.

RED CHILLIES

Dried red chillies give a very good flavour, and I would not hesitate to use them in place of fresh. They are slightly sweeter than fresh red chillies. Green chillies are hotter and not available in dried form.

STEP 2

STEP 3

STEP 4

STEP 5

VINDALOO CURRY

Vindaloo is the classic fiery curry that originates in Goa. The 'vin' in the title refers to the vinegar that is added to tenderize the meat. The vinegar has to be balanced with other flavours, such as chilli, and does not work so well with any meat other than pork.

SERVES 4–6

100 ml/ 3½ fl oz/ scant ½ cup oil
1 large onion, sliced into half rings
120 ml/4 fl oz/½ cup white wine vinegar
300 ml/½ pint/1¼ cups water
750 g/ 1½ lb boneless pork shoulder, diced
2 tsp cumin seeds
4 dried red chillies
1 tsp black peppercorns
6 green cardamom pods
2.5 cm/1 inch piece cinnamon stick
1 tsp black mustard seeds
3 cloves
1 tsp fenugreek seeds
2 tbsp ghee
4 garlic cloves, chopped finely
3.5 cm/1½ inch piece ginger root, chopped finely
1 tbsp coriander seeds, ground
2 tomatoes, peeled and chopped
250 g/8 oz potato, cut into 1 cm/½ inch cubes
1 tsp light brown sugar
½ tsp ground turmeric
salt

TO SERVE:
basmati rice
pickles

1 Heat the oil in a large saucepan and fry the onion until golden brown. Set aside.

2 Combine 2 tablespoons of the vinegar with 1 tablespoon of the water in a large bowl, add the pork and stir together well. Set aside.

3 In a food processor or blender mix the onions, cumin, chillies, peppercorns, cardamom, cinnamon, mustard seeds, cloves and fenugreek to a paste. Alternatively, grind the ingredients together in a pestle and mortar. Transfer to a bowl and add the remaining vinegar.

4 Heat the ghee in a frying pan (skillet) or casserole and cook the pork until it is browned on all sides.

5 Stir in the garlic, ginger and ground coriander until fragrant, then add the tomatoes, potato, brown sugar, turmeric and remaining water. Add salt to taste and bring to the boil. Stir in the spice paste, cover and reduce the heat, and simmer for 1 hour until the pork is tender.

6 Serve with basmati rice and pickles.

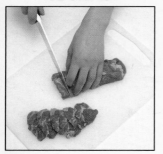

STEP 1

STEP 2

STEP 4

STEP 5

MASALA KEBABS

Indian kebab dishes are not necessarily cooked on a skewer; they can also be served in a dish and are always dry dishes with no sauce. This is an extremely tasty, simply flavoured dish, using a traditional masala mix.

SERVES 4–6

750 g/ 1½ lb lamb neck fillet
1 dried bay leaf
2.5 cm/ 1 inch piece ginger root, chopped
2.5 cm/ 1 inch cinnamon stick
1 tsp coriander seeds
½ tsp salt
1 tsp fennel seeds
1 tsp chilli powder
1 tsp Garam Masala (see page 76)
1 tsp lemon juice
1 tsp ground turmeric
1 tbsp oil

TO GARNISH:
fresh coriander (cilantro) sprigs
lemon wedges

TO SERVE:
bread
chutney

1 Cut the lamb into 5mm/¼inch slices.

2 Use a food processor, blender or pestle and mortar to grind together the bay leaf, ginger, cinnamon, coriander seeds, salt, fennel seeds and chilli powder.

3 Combine this spice mix with the garam masala, lemon juice, turmeric and oil in a large bowl.

4 Add the lamb to the spice mix and leave to marinate at room temperature for about 1 hour, or in the refrigerator for 3 hours or overnight.

5 Spread out the pieces of lamb on a baking sheet and cook in a preheated oven at 200°C/400°F/Gas mark 6 for 20 minutes until well done. Transfer to paper towels to drain any excess fat.

6 Thread 3 or 4 pieces of meat on to each skewer and garnish with fresh coriander (cilantro) sprigs and lemon wedges. Serve hot with bread and chutney.

BARBECUE DISH

This dish is ideal for a barbecue, to serve while the main dish is being cooked; the little morsels with their strong flavours and small size will keep appetites keen. Thread the marinated pieces of meat on to soaked wooden skewers, or oiled metal skewers, and cook over a hot barbecue.

CHAPTER FOUR

Fish Dishes

There is a vast array of fresh seafood in southern India, Bengal, Calcutta and its environs, and as far north as Darjeeling. North of Calcutta rivers and streams flow from the Himalayas. The water is very clean and pure and a great variety of river fish is caught. Lake fish are also enjoyed when available.

The same varieties of fish cannot be readily obtained in the West, but I have adapted the recipes for fish that can be bought more easily. However, if you are ever near an Indian supermarket, it is worth a look in just to see the amazing variety of warm water fish that is frozen and exported from India, such as huge catfish, pomfret, eels and enormous uncooked prawns (shrimp). Lake and river fish are also exported, and such well-known fish as carp, perch, pike and baby eels (elvers) are readily available.

Although fresh uncooked tiger prawns (shrimp) are usually expensive, frozen packs of them can be found in most supermarkets and freezer stores, and it is these that I have used in the prawn (shrimp) recipes because they have more flavour and are more versatile than ready-cooked prawns (shrimp).

Opposite: *Palms sway in the breeze on Anjuna beach in Goa.*

STEP 1

STEP 2

STEP 3

STEP 4

GREEN FISH CURRY

This dish is from southern India. It has a wonderful fresh, hot, exotic taste resulting from the generous amount of fresh herbs, sharp fresh chillies and coconut milk.

SERVES 4

1 tbsp oil
2 spring onions (scallions), sliced
1 tsp cumin seeds, ground
2 fresh green chillies, choppped
1 tsp coriander seeds, ground
4 tbsp chopped fresh coriander (cilantro)
4 tbsp chopped fresh mint
1 tbsp chopped chives
150 ml / $^{1}/_{4}$ pint/$^{2}/_{3}$ cup coconut milk
4 white fish fillets, about 250 g/8 oz each
salt and pepper

TO SERVE:
basmati rice
mint to garnish

1 Heat the oil in a large frying pan (skillet) or shallow saucepan and add the spring onions (scallions).

2 Stir-fry the spring onions (scallions) over a medium heat until they are softened but not coloured. Stir in the cumin, chillies and ground coriander, and cook them until fragrant.

3 Add the fresh coriander (cilantro), mint, chives and coconut milk and season liberally.

4 Carefully place the fish in the pan and poach for 10–15 minutes until the flesh flakes when tested with a fork. Serve the fish fillets in the sauce with basmati rice.

FISH

Any white fish can be used for this dish. In most supermarkets a wide range of frozen fish is available; it is cheaper than fresh fish and is fine for this dish because the flavour of the fish is not as important as the sauce it is cooked in.

STEP 1

STEP 2

STEP 3

STEP 4

PRAWN (SHRIMP) DANSAK

Parsis are, in the context of India's history, relatively new, having arrived only 500 years ago. The Parsi cuisine favours elaborate preparations, usually done by the household cooks. The lentil purée sauce in this recipe is of Parsi origin and popular throughout India.

SERVES 4–6

750 g/1¹/₂ lb uncooked tiger prawns
   (shrimp) in their shells or 650 g/1 lb 5 oz
   peeled tiger prawns (shrimp), or cooked,
   peeled Atlantic prawns (shrimp)
1 tsp salt
1 dried bay leaf
3 garlic cloves
90 g/3 oz/¹/₃ cup split yellow peas, soaked
   for 1 hour in cold water and drained
60 g/2 oz/¹/₄ cup red lentils
1 carrot, chopped
1 potato, cut into large dice
3 tbsp drained canned sweetcorn
3 tbsp oil
2 onions, chopped
¹/₂ tsp yellow mustard seeds
1¹/₂ tsp coriander seeds, ground
¹/₂ tsp cumin seeds, ground
¹/₂ tsp fenugreek seeds, ground
1¹/₂ tsp ground turmeric
1 dried red chilli
425 g/14 oz can tomatoes
¹/₂ tsp Garam Masala (see page 76)
3 tbsp chopped fresh coriander (cilantro)
2 tbsp chopped fresh mint

1 Reserve a few of the prawns (shrimp) for garnish and peel the rest. Set aside. Cook those for the garnish in boiling water for 3–5 minutes.

2 Fill a large saucepan with water and add the salt, bay leaf, 1 garlic clove and the split yellow peas. Bring to the boil and cook for 15 minutes. Add the red lentils, carrot and potato and cook, uncovered, for a further 15 minutes. Drain, discarding the garlic and bay leaf.

3 Purée the cooked vegetables with the sweetcorn in a blender or food processor. Alternatively, use a potato masher to break down the lumps.

4 Crush the remaining garlic. Heat the oil in a large saucepan and cook the onion and garlic for 3–4 minutes. Add the mustard seeds and when they start to pop, stir in the ground coriander, cumin, fenugreek, turmeric and chilli. Add the peeled prawns (shrimp) and stir over a high heat for 1–2 minutes.

5 Add the tomatoes and the puréed vegetables, and gently simmer. Cook, uncovered, for 30–40 minutes. Stir in the garam masala and taste for seasoning.

6 Serve, sprinkled with the fresh coriander (cilantro) and mint, and garnished with reserved prawns (shrimp).

STEP 1

STEP 1

STEP 2

STEP 4

MASALA FRIED FISH

Frying fish is classically Indian, although it does not always spring to mind when thinking of Indian food.

SERVES 4–8

*8 plaice or other white fish fillets, about
   125–150 g/4–5 oz each
1 tbsp ground turmeric
2 tbsp plain (all-purpose) flour
salt
1/2 tsp black peppercorns, ground
1 tsp chilli powder
1 tbsp coriander seeds, ground
1 garlic clove, crushed
2 tsp Garam Masala (see page 76)
oil for deep frying*

*TO GARNISH:
chilli powder
lemon wedges*

1 To skin the fish fillets, lay the fillet skin side down with the tail nearest you. Hold the tail end between your thumb and forefinger. Hold a sharp knife at a shallow angle to the fish in your other hand. Holding the fish firmly, make an angled cut between the flesh and the skin, then continue to cut the flesh away from the skin until it is free.

2 In a shallow dish, combine the turmeric, flour, salt, peppercorns, chilli powder, coriander seeds, garlic and garam masala. Mix well.

3 Fill a shallow saucepan or a deep frying pan (skillet) with oil to a depth of 5–7 cm/2–3 inches, and heat to 180° C/350° F.

4 Coat the fish fillets in the spice mix either by shaking gently in a paper bag or turning over in the dish of spice mix until well coated.

5 Deep fry the fish fillets for about 3–5 minutes, turning often until the fish flakes with a fork. Drain on plenty of paper towels.

6 Serve sprinkled with chilli powder, garnished with lemon wedges, and accompanied by a selection of pickles and chutneys.

DEEP FRYING

When deep frying, it is important to use oil at the correct temperature. If the oil is too hot, the outside of the food will burn, as will the spices, before the inside is cooked. If the oil is too cool, the food will be sodden with oil before a crisp crust forms. Draining on paper towels is essential, as they absorb excess oil and moisture.

STEP 1

STEP 2

STEP 3

STEP 4

PRAWN (SHRIMP) BHUNA

This is a fiery recipe with subtle undertones. As the flavour of the prawns should be noticeable, the spices should not take over this dish. The term 'Bhuna' refers to the method of bringing out the full flavours of the spices by heating them in a pan before adding the other ingredients.

SERVES 4–6

2 dried red chillies, deseeded if liked
3 fresh green chillies, finely chopped
1 tsp ground turmeric
2 tsp white wine vinegar
$^{1}/_{2}$ tsp salt
3 garlic cloves, crushed
$^{1}/_{2}$ tsp ground black pepper
1 tsp paprika
500 g/ 1 lb uncooked peeled king prawns
  (shrimp)
4 tbsp oil
1 onion, chopped very finely
180 ml/ 6 fl oz/ $^{3}/_{4}$ cup water
2 tbsp lemon juice
2 tsp Garam Masala (see page 76)
fresh coriander (cilantro) sprigs to garnish

1 Combine the chillies, turmeric, vinegar, salt, garlic, pepper and paprika in a non-metallic bowl. Stir in the prawns and set aside for 10 minutes.

2 Heat the oil in a large frying pan (skillet) or wok, add the onion and fry for 3–4 minutes until the onion is soft.

3 Add the prawns (shrimp) and the contents of the bowl to the pan and stir-fry over a high heat for 2 minutes.

4 Reduce the heat, add the water and boil for 10 minutes, stirring occasionally, until the water is evaporated and the curry is fragrant.

5 Stir in the lemon juice and garam masala.

6 Serve garnished with fresh coriander (cilantro) sprigs.

FLAVOUR FROM HERBS AND SPICES

To get the full flavour from any spices they must be heated first. This also applies to dried herbs. To make raita with dried herbs, take 3 tsp of dried mint and put it into a dry pan, warm it through very gently until you can start to smell the mint. Remove it from the heat and add 120 ml/4 fl oz/½ cup natural yogurt and salt to taste. Transfer to a serving dish.

PRAWN (SHRIMP) BIRIANI

Like Lamb Biriani (see page 16), this dish is usually served on special occasions because it needs close attention during cooking. However, the flavours are more subtle than those of Lamb Biriani, so it is a lighter dish and more suitable for every day.

STEP 3

SERVES 6–8

250 g/8 oz/generous 1 cup basmati rice, rinsed and drained
1 tsp saffron strands
50 ml/2 fl oz/4 tbsp tepid water
2 shallots, chopped coarsely
3 garlic cloves, crushed
1 tsp chopped ginger root
2 tsp coriander seeds
1/2 tsp black peppercorns
2 cloves
2 green cardamom pods
2.5 cm/1 inch piece cinnamon stick
1 tsp ground turmeric
1 fresh green chilli, chopped
1/2 tsp salt
2 tbsp ghee
1 tsp whole black mustard seeds
500 g/1 lb uncooked tiger prawns (shrimp) in their shells, or 425 g/14 oz peeled uncooked tiger prawns (shrimp), or cooked and peeled Atlantic prawns (shrimp)
300 ml/1/2 pint/1 1/4 cups coconut milk
300 ml/1/2 pint/1 1/4 cups natural yogurt
1 tbsp sultanas (golden raisins)

TO GARNISH:
3 tbsp flaked (slivered) almonds, toasted
1 spring onion (scallion), sliced and rinsed

1 Soak the rice in cold water for 2 hours. Combine the saffron with the tepid water and soak for 10 minutes.

2 Put the shallots, garlic, ginger, coriander, peppercorns, cloves, cardamom, cinnamon, turmeric, chilli and salt into a spice blender or pestle and mortar and grind to a paste.

STEP 3

3 Heat the ghee in a large saucepan and add the mustard seeds. When they start to pop, add the prawns (shrimp) and stir over a high heat for 1 minute. Stir in the spice mix, then the coconut milk and yogurt. Simmer for 20 minutes.

STEP 4

4 Meanwhile, bring a large saucepan of salted water to the boil. Drain the rice and slowly add to the pan. Boil for 12 minutes. Drain. Carefully pile the rice on the prawns. Spoon over the sultanas (golden raisins) and trickle the saffron and water over the rice in lines.

5 Cover the pan with a clean tea towel or dish towel and put the lid on tightly. Remove the pan from heat and leave to stand for 5 minutes to infuse. Serve, garnished with the toasted almonds and spring onion (scallion).

STEP 5

STEP 1

STEP 2

STEP 3

STEP 4

CURRIED CRAB

Shellfish is a major part of the diet in coastal areas of India. It is frozen and shipped to all parts India, and all over the world where there is a large Indian community. In India tiny crabs are used in fish dishes, like those used in the South of France. These crabs are not always widely available, so I have used the more common Edible Crab (Cancer pagrus).

SERVES 4

2 tbsp mustard oil
1 tbsp ghee
1 onion, chopped finely
5 cm/2 inch piece ginger root, grated
2 garlic cloves, peeled but left whole
1 tsp ground turmeric
1 tsp salt
1 tsp chilli powder
2 fresh green chillies, chopped
1 tsp paprika
125 g/4 oz/½ cup brown crab meat
350 g/12 oz/1½ cups white crab meat
250 ml/8 fl oz /1 cup natural yogurt
1 tsp Garam Masala (see page 76)

TO SERVE:
basmati rice
fresh coriander (cilantro) to garnish

1 Heat the mustard oil in a large, preferably non-stick, frying pan (skillet), wok or saucepan. When it starts to smoke add the ghee and onion. Stir for 3 minutes over a medium heat until the onion is soft.

2 Stir in the ginger and whole garlic cloves.

3 Add the turmeric, salt, chilli powder, chillies and paprika. Stir to mix thoroughly.

4 Increase the heat and add the crab meat and yogurt. Simmer, stirring occasionally, for 10 minutes until the sauce is thickened slightly. Add garam masala to taste.

5 Serve hot, over plain basmati rice, with the fresh coriander (cilantro) either chopped or in sprigs.

CRAB MEAT

If you cannot buy fresh crab meat, frozen crab meat is a good substitute. It can be bought frozen in packs, which usually contain half brown meat and half white meat. Use canned crab meat as a last resort, as it has less flavour.

CHAPTER FIVE

Vegetable Dishes

By applying myriad methods born of a centuries-old tradition of vegetarianism, Indian cooks turn the simplest vegetables into the most extraordinary feasts. Many of these cooking methods are completely alien to us, but they result in dishes which are both a joy to eat and nourishing to mind and body.

Indian vegetarianism is due mainly to the predominant Hindu religion, with its reverence for animals – especially cows – and its ideal of harmonizing the diet with the needs of the soul. A vegetarian diet is also followed because vegetable cropping is a more efficient use of land than keeping animals for food.

Although we may be used to eating vegetables with Indian meals in restaurants, restaurant cuisine here differs markedly from native cuisine. In India vegetables are relied on to play a leading role in a meal, for example, in a *bhaji* (a dry curry), or puréed in a *bhartha*.

Vegetable curries are flavoured simply and the spices and sauces can be transferred easily between vegetables. For example, the flavourings in one dal stew can easily be used with other available pulses, the sauce Palak Paneer (see page 72) can be used with other leafy vegetables, and your own spice mixes experimented with when you have some vegetables to cook.

Opposite: *Farmers threshing rice with oxen at a farm in Nepal.*

STEP 1

STEP 2

STEP 3

STEP 4

CHANNA DAL

This is a dish to consider next time you wish to prepare a dal. Many types of dal, dried pulses and lentils, are used in India, but fewer are available elsewhere. Dals can be cooked in similar ways, but the soaking and cooking times do vary, so check the pack for instructions.

SERVES 4–6

2 tbsp ghee
1 large onion, chopped finely
1 garlic clove, crushed
1 tbsp grated ginger root
1 tbsp cumin seeds, ground
2 tsp coriander seeds, ground
1 dried red chilli
2.5 cm/1 inch piece cinnamon stick
1 tsp salt
$^1/_2$ tsp ground turmeric
250 g/$^1/_2$ lb/1 cup split yellow peas, soaked
  in cold water for 1 hour and drained
425 g/14 oz can plum tomatoes
300 ml/$^1/_2$ pint/1$^1/_4$ cups water
2 tsp Garam Masala (see page 76)

1 Heat the ghee in a large saucepan, add the onion, garlic and ginger and fry for 3–4 minutes until the onion has softened slightly.

2 Add the cumin, coriander, chilli, cinnamon, salt and turmeric, then stir in the split peas until well mixed.

3 Add the contents of the can of tomatoes, breaking the tomatoes up slightly with the back of the spoon.

4 Add the water and bring to the boil. Reduce the heat to very low and simmer, uncovered, for about 40 minutes, stirring occasionally, until most of the liquid has been absorbed and the split peas are tender. Skim the surface occasionally with a perforated spoon to remove any scum.

5 Gradually stir in the garam masala, tasting after each addition, until it is of the required flavour.

HANDY HINTS

Use a non-stick saucepan if you have one, because the mixture is quite dense and does stick to a pan at the bottom occasionally. If the dal is overstirred the split peas will break up and the dish will not have much texture or bite.

STEP 1

STEP 2

STEP 3

STEP 3

TARKA DAL

*This is just one version of many dals that are served throughout India;
in the absence of regular supplies of meat, they form a
staple part of the diet.*

SERVES 4

2 tbsp ghee
2 shallots, sliced
1 tsp yellow mustard seeds
2 garlic cloves, crushed
8 fenugreek seeds
1 cm/^{1}/$_2$ inch piece ginger root, grated
^{1}/$_2$ tsp salt
125 g/4 oz/^{1}/$_2$ cup red lentils
1 tbsp tomato purée (paste)
600 ml/1 pint/2^1/$_2$ cups water
2 tomatoes, peeled and chopped
1 tbsp lemon juice
4 tbsp chopped fresh coriander (cilantro)
^{1}/$_2$ tsp chilli powder
^{1}/$_2$ tsp Garam Masala (see page 76)
naan bread to serve

1 Heat half of the ghee in a large saucepan, and add the shallots. Cook for 2–3 minutes over a high heat, then add the mustard seeds. Cover the pan until the seeds begin to pop.

2 Immediately remove the lid from the pan and add the garlic, fenugreek, ginger and salt.

3 Stir once and add the lentils, tomato purée (paste) and water and simmer gently for 10 minutes.

4 Stir in the tomatoes, lemon juice, and coriander (cilantro) and simmer for a further 4–5 minutes until the lentils are tender.

5 Transfer to a serving dish. Heat the remaining ghee in a small saucepan until it starts to bubble. Remove from the heat and stir in the garam masala and chilli powder. Immediately pour over the tarka dal and serve.

DALS

The flavours in a dal can be altered to suit your personal taste; for example, for added heat, add more chilli powder or chillies, or add fennel seeds for a pleasant aniseed flavour.

To make a dal stew into a single-dish meal, add a combination of vegetables, such as fried aubergine cubes (eggplant), courgettes (zucchini), carrots, or any firm vegetable that you have to hand; pumpkin is particularly successful.

ALOO CHAT

Aloo Chat (chat means salad) is one of a variety of Indian foods served at any time of the day. Indians are expert at combining flavours and textures in subtle mixes designed to satisfy and stimulate the appetite.

SERVES 4

125 g/4 oz/generous ¹/₂ cup chick-peas
(garbanzo beans), soaked overnight in cold
water and drained
1 dried red chilli
500 g/1 lb waxy potatoes, such as red-
skinned or Cyprus potatoes, boiled in their
skins and peeled
1 tsp cumin seeds
1 tsp black peppercorns
2 tsp salt
¹/₂ tsp dried mint
¹/₂ tsp chilli powder
¹/₂ tsp ground ginger
2 tsp mango powder
120 ml/4 fl oz/¹/₂ cup natural yogurt
oil for deep frying
4 poppadoms

TO SERVE:
Cucumber Raita (see page 26)

1 Boil the chick-peas (garbanzo beans) with the chilli in plenty of water for about 1 hour until tender. Drain.

2 Cut the potatoes into 2.5 cm/ 1 inch dice and mix into the chick-peas (garbanzo beans) while they are still warm. Set aside.

3 Grind together the cumin, peppercorns and salt in a spice grinder or pestle and mortar. Stir in the mint, chilli powder, ginger and mango powder.

4 Put a small dry saucepan or frying pan (skillet) over a low heat and add the spice mix. Stir until fragrant and immediately remove from the heat.

5 Stir half of the spice mix into the chick-peas (garbanzo beans) and potatoes, and stir the yogurt into the other half.

6 Cook the poppadoms according to the pack instructions. Drain on plenty of paper towels. Break into bite-size pieces and stir into the potatoes and chick-peas (garbanzo beans), spoon over the spiced yogurt and serve with the cucumber raita.

VARIATION

Instead of chick-peas (garbanzo beans), diced tropical fruits can be stirred into the potatoes and spice mix; add a little lemon juice to balance the sweetness.

STEP 1

STEP 2

STEP 3

STEP 4

STEP 2

STEP 2

STEP 3

STEP 4

BOMBAY POTATOES

Although virtually unknown in India, this dish is a very popular item on Indian restaurant menus in other parts of the world. It works best when served with rice as a vegetable dish, rather than instead of rice. The success of the recipe rests on using waxy potatoes such as red-skinned or Cyprus potatoes, because they do not break up readily.

SERVES 4

1 kg/2 lb waxy potatoes, peeled
2 tbsp ghee
1 tsp panch poran spice mix (see below)
3 tsp ground turmeric
2 tbsp tomato purée (paste)
300 ml/¹/₂ pint/1¹/₄ cups natural yogurt
salt
chopped fresh coriander (cilantro) to garnish

1 Put the whole potatoes into a large saucepan of salted cold water, bring to the boil, then simmer until the potatoes are just cooked but not tender; the time depends on the size of the potato, but an average-sized one should take about 15 minutes.

2 Put the ghee into a saucepan over a medium heat, and add the panch poran, turmeric, tomato purée (paste), yogurt and salt. Bring to the boil, and simmer, uncovered, for 5 minutes.

3 Drain the potatoes and cut each into 4 pieces.

4 Add the potatoes to the pan and cook with a lid on. Transfer to an ovenproof casserole, cover and cook in a preheated oven at 180°C/350°F/Gas

mark 4 for about 40 minutes, until the potatoes are tender and the sauce has thickened a little.

5 Sprinkle liberally with fresh chopped coriander (cilantro) and serve immediately.

PANCH PORAN SPICE MIX

Panch poran spice mix can be bought from Asian or Indian grocery stores, or make your own from equal quantities of cumin seeds, fennel seeds, mustard seeds, nigella seeds and fenugreek seeds.

BOILING VEGETABLES

Cooking vegetables and rice in water at a rolling boil does not speed the cooking, and when cooking potatoes it just ensures that they break up and quickly go to a mush. Unless a recipe specifies a rolling boil, I recommend keeping the water at a simmer once it has come up to the boil initially.

STEP 1

STEP 2

STEP 3

STEP 4

PALAK PANEER

Paneer, curd cheese, figures widely on Indian menus. It is combined with all sorts of ingredients, but most popularly with spinach and vegetables. In this recipe, paneer is combined with spices and a sauce for a dish which is a favourite with vegetarians, but is so delicious it is often served as an accompaniment to a curry.

SERVES 4–6

2 tbsp ghee
1 onion, sliced
1 garlic clove, crushed
1 dried red chilli
1 tsp ground turmeric
500 g/1 lb waxy potatoes, such as red-
   skinned or Cyprus potatoes, cut into 2.5
   cm/1 inch cubes
425 g/14 oz can tomatoes, drained
150 ml/¼ pint/⅔ cup water
250 g/8 oz/6 cups fresh spinach
500 g/1 lb/2 cups curd cheese, cut into 2.5
   cm/1 inch cubes
1 tsp Garam Masala (see page 76)
1 tbsp chopped fresh coriander (cilantro)
1 tbsp chopped fresh parsley
salt and pepper
naan bread to serve

1 Heat the ghee in a saucepan, add the onion and cook over a low heat for 10 minutes until very soft. Add the garlic and chilli and cook for a further 5 minutes.

2 Add the turmeric, salt, potatoes, tomatoes and water and bring to the boil.

3 Simmer for 10–15 minutes until the potatoes are cooked.

4 Stir in the spinach, cheese cubes, garam masala, coriander (cilantro) and parsley to taste.

5 Simmer for a further 5 minutes and season well. Serve with naan bread.

CURD CHEESE

Indian *paneer* is a homemade fresh cheese. It is very simple to make: into a large saucepan pour 2.25 litres/4 pints/2½ quarts of very creamy milk. Heat until the surface of the milk is quivering, stirring occasionally to prevent the milk from catching on the bottom of the pan. Remove the pan from the heat and add 4 tablespoons of vinegar. *Do not stir.* The milk will separate. When it is quite cool, pour the separated milk through a clean tea towel, and tie up the remaining solids in the cloth. Put on a draining board, cover with a strong board and stand a heavy weight on top (I usually use several food cans, or a large saucepan full of water). Leave for at least 4 hours to squeeze out the water and to leave you with a cheese that you can cut into 2.5 cm/1 inch cubes.

Fresh Italian pecorino cheese can be used as a substitute.

STEP 1

STEP 2

STEP 4

STEP 5

BRINDIL BHAJI

This is one of the most delicious of the bhaji dishes, and has a wonderful sweet spicy flavour.

SERVES 4

500 g/1 lb aubergines (eggplant), cut into 1
    cm/¹/₂ inch slices
2 tbsp ghee
1 onion, thinly sliced
2 garlic cloves, sliced
2.5 cm/1 inch piece ginger root, grated
¹/₂ tsp ground turmeric
1 dried red chilli
¹/₂ tsp salt
425 g/14 oz can tomatoes
1 tsp Garam Masala (see page 76)
fresh coriander (cilantro) sprigs to garnish

1 Cut the aubergine (eggplant) slices into finger-width strips using a sharp knife.

2 Heat the ghee in a saucepan and cook the onion over a medium heat for 7–8 minutes, stirring constantly, until very soft.

3 Add the garlic and aubergine (eggplant), increase the heat and cook for 2 minutes.

4 Stir in the ginger, the turmeric, chilli, salt and the contents of the can of tomatoes. Use the back of a wooden spoon to break up the tomatoes.

Simmer uncovered for 15–20 minutes until the aubergine (eggplant) is very soft.

5 Make the garam masala (see page 76) and then stir in. Simmer for a further 4–5 minutes.

6 Serve garnished with fresh coriander (cilantro) sprigs.

VARIATION

Other vegetables can be used instead of the aubergines (eggplants). Try courgettes (zucchini), potatoes or (bell) peppers, or any combination of these vegetables, using the same sauce.

74

INDIAN CUISINE

All Indian spice blends are called *masalas*, such as garam masala, chat masala, or hara masala. In Indian households, spice blends are freshly ground as and when needed, and if you want to make your own they will keep for a couple of months in an airtight jar in a cool, dark, dry place.

Garam Masala

This is the recipe for Garam Masala that has been used in this book:

1 tsp cardamom seeds
2 tsp cloves
2 tbsp cumin seeds
2 tbsp coriander seeds
2 dried bay leaves
7.5 cm/ 3 inch piece cinnamon
  stick
1 tbsp black peppercorns
1 dried red chilli

1. Grind the spices and the bay leaves together in a spice grinder or pestle and mortar until the aromas are released. Use as required.

If there is one thing which defines classic Indian cooking, it is the use of spices to flavour food, and the Indian masterchef has perfected all the techniques that make the Indian repertoire full of subtleties, deep flavours and harmonized combinations.

MASTERING THE ART

Any cook with more than 30 spices to choose from has to be sure of what he or she is doing, which only comes with experience, and that with practice. It is a bit like planning an outfit: you just have to try different combinations until one works! So roll up your sleeves and start, with a dal (see pages 64 and 66), I suggest, as the flavour of the spices really comes through. I will try to open the door on the subject of herbs and spices, and explain how to get the most out of them.

You do not have to start off with a vast array of spices, just six or seven basic ones which can be added to at any time as your recipe repertoire expands.

DRIED SPICES

Seeds

The majority of dried spices used in Indian cooking are seeds, including nigella or black onion seeds, fennel seeds, sesame seeds, dill seeds, peppercorns, cumin seeds, coriander seeds, poppy seeds, cardamom seeds, caraway seeds ajowan seeds and fenugreek seeds. Seeds are used both whole and ground.

Buying and storing dried spices

I always go to an Asian or Indian store for my spices, as they can be bought far more cheaply there than in other food shops and supermarkets. Asian and Indian stores also have a high turnover so their spices should be fresh. If possible, buy whole spices and grind them as you need them. Do not buy packs of spices, either whole or ground, that have dust or powder in the bottom, and check the sell-by date.

Whole spices will keep for up to one year if stored in a cool, dark, dry place. If you do buy ground spices, ideally use them immediately, or at least use them within 3 months because their flavour rapidly deteriorates if kept for longer. Avoid allowing spices to become too warm or leaving them exposed to light as the flavour will quickly fade.

Grinding dried spices

When you are grinding dried spices, you do not have to reduce them to a powder. As soon as the seed is broken it starts to give out the aromatic oil which contains the flavour. This oil quickly goes rancid, so commercially ground seeds have to be dried, losing much of their flavour along the way.

I use a spice mill or coffee grinder for grinding spices so that I can whip up freshly ground spice mixes in a jiffy. Alternatively, you could use a pestle and mortar.

For the recipes in this book, I have used freshly ground spices, and I know that once you have started cooking with these you will find it very difficult to go back to the ready-ground versions. Not only are the freshly ground spices noticeably more aromatic, but the strength of their flavour is more consistent.

Cooking with dried spices

To coax the flavour and colour from dried spices and give dishes a pleasant, harmonized flavour, a number of different techniques are used in Indian cooking.

The most popular method is *bhun-na,* in which the spices are either roasted or fried. To roast the spices, put them into a frying pan (skillet) set over a low heat; I always put a lid on the pan because the heat tends to excite some spices, especially seeds like mustard seeds which are used whole, so much that you may find they jump out of the pan. Shake the pan continuously until the spices are fragrant. The spices are now ready to use. When the spices are fried, they can either be added to hot oil or ghee, or heated at the same time as the fat. They are then fried until they are fragrant.

Another method of bringing out the flavour of spices is called *bhaghar.* For this, whole spices are added to hot ghee or oil in a pan and fried until they are golden brown. The whole contents of the pan are poured, sizzling hot, on top of a prepared dish, such as meat, poultry, vegetables, fish or pulses, and the lid is immediately put back on to keep all the aroma in while the spices infuse. This method is especially popular with dals, as it adds a delicious richness and flavour to the dish.

FRESH SPICES

Ginger and garlic

The flavours of both ginger and garlic can be changed according to how they are prepared. For instance, a whole garlic clove added to a dish will give it the flavour but not the 'bite' of the garlic; a halved clove will add a little bite, while a finely chopped garlic clove will release most of the flavour, and a crushed clove will release all of the flavour. I save the crushed version for the weekend! Roasting a whole head of garlic sweetens the flavour incredibly, and gives it an extra dimension. It also takes away some of the sourness, so that roasted garlic can be used with more confidence than raw garlic.

If you are making a spice blend in a food processor or blender, both ginger and garlic can be ground with the other spices. If you are using a pestle and mortar to make the blend, coarsely chop the ginger and garlic before grinding them with the spices.

Ginger and garlic burn very quickly if overheated, so I only use a medium heat when cooking them initially. However, garlic is sometimes browned intentionally for its smoky flavour, which will permeate a whole dish and should be used judiciously.

Chillies

Chillies deserve a whole chapter to themselves; in fact there are a number of books available solely on chillies. However, I will say little more here than that, generally, if they are small they are hot, if they are big they are not!

Green Masala

This green masala is particularly fresh-tasting and terrific when used to pep up a rice salad, or stirred into hot rice just before serving.

2.5 cm/1 in piece fresh ginger root, peeled and chopped
1 garlic clove
4 green chillies
4 tbsp coriander (cilantro) leaves and stalks, chopped
water
pinch salt

1. Peel and chop the ginger root and garlic clove. Remove the seeds from the green chillies and slice them.

2. Put all the ingredients into a pestle and mortar and pound, adding a little water as required to make a paste.

3. Use as required, adding a little at a time to taste.

Sri Lankan Curry Powder

The ingredients of this spice blend are roasted before being ground to give it a deliciously nutty, smoky aroma.

1 tbsp fennel seeds
1 tsp fenugreek seeds
2.5 cm/1 inch piece cinnamon
6 green cardamom pods
6 cloves
3 tbsp coriander seeds
2 tbsp cumin seeds
6 curry leaves, dried or fresh
1/2 tsp chilli powder

1. Put the fennel seeds, fenugreek seeds, cinnamon, cardamom pods, cloves, coriander seeds and cumin seeds in a dry frying pan (skillet). Roast over medium heat, stirring constantly until the spices turn a rich dark brown.

2. Spread the spices out on to a plate to cool. Add the curry leaves and chilli powder.

3. Put all the ingredients into a pestle and mortar and grind well to produce a fine powder.

4. Use as required, as soon as possible, as the blend loses its aroma after a week or two.

The chilli plant is a member of the capsicum family, which is native to Central and South America and the West Indies. Two hundred or more varieties of chillies are grown around the world. They may be green, red, orange, yellow or purple. They are available fresh, dried, flaked, crushed and ground. However, when buying chilli powder make sure that it is pure ground chillies, and not a blend of spices.

Different varieties of chillies are used in different countries. In India the most popular variety is the red, 12.5 cm/ 5 inch long cayenne chilli, which can be bought fresh or dried. Other varieties of chilli you may see include the habanero chilli, which is a small, bitingly hot lantern-shaped chilli from the West Indies, and the extremely hot, tiny red bird's eye chilli from Thailand. Also common are serrano chillies, which are green, stubby chillies, about 7.5 cm/ 3 inches long and generally available in supermarkets. The very long green chillies that you may have seen, up to 15 cm/6 inches long, which are called anaheim, are relatively mild.

The heat in a chilli is contained in a substance called capsaicin, which is found predominantly in the seeds, and is also present in the veins and the skin. So to lessen the heat of a chilli, remove the seeds, and then the veins. Alternatively, leave the chilli whole and remove it before the end of the cooking time.

Some chillies can be very fiery and in large quantities can cause intestinal damage, or at the least a very sore mouth. Pulses, rice and bread dilute the heat, but water will only intensify it.

When using chillies, always err on the side of caution. More can be added to make a sauce hotter but it is more difficult to reduce the heat, which is why I always add chillies gradually, tasting after each addition. If you do find that you have made a dish too hot, you can tame the fire by adding an ingredient such as potatoes or lentils.

Chillies can also be added to dishes as a condiment in various forms, such as chilli sauce, pepper sauce and chilli oil. However, I have found that brands vary from sweet to vinegary, so you may have to experiment to find one to your taste.

New forms of spices

A last word about the use of spices – several new forms are available, such as oils, powders and essences. These are fine to substitute for the real thing, but do bear in mind that freshly ground spices have the best flavour, and anything else is a substitute.

HERBS

Herbs are added to Indian dishes to balance the spices and to add freshness to a dish. The main herbs used in Indian cooking are fresh coriander (cilantro) and parsley, which are always used fresh rather than dried.

Leaves

Leaves, such as bay leaves, can be used fresh or dried and either whole or ground into a blend. Some fresh leaves, like bay leaves, can be quite strong, so you may like to remove them before the end of the cooking time for a milder taste.

Buying and storing herbs

Fresh herbs are widely available in packets, bunches and growing in pots, in supermarkets, grocery stores and greengrocers, and many are easy to grow in a garden or window box.

Try to buy herbs in bunches, as they are usually more hardy and better value than herbs in packets. At their freshest, herbs should be perky with firm stalks and leaves; as they age they dehydrate and become limp. To store bunches of herbs, wash any dirt from them, rinse well and put them up to their leaves in a jar of cold water. If possible, store them like this in the refrigerator, although they can be kept at room temperature if necessary. For extra crispness, and to revive limp herbs, rinse them in cold water and shake off any excess, then store overnight in an airtight container in the refrigerator. Pots of growing herbs need plenty of water, and should be stored in the door of the refrigerator.

If fresh herbs are not available, dried or frozen herbs, or herb oils can be used instead. When buying dried herbs, look for the freeze-dried type, which are widely available, because they are dried very quickly and have a better flavour than traditionally dried herbs. Avoid buying dried herbs that have a lot of powder or dust in the pack, as the chances are that the quality will not be very good.

Store dried herbs and herb oils in a cool, dark, dry place.

Cooking with herbs

With a lot of the softer fresh herbs, such as parsley and fresh coriander (cilantro), the stalks as well as the leaves provide flavour, although they usually taste less sweet. Chop stalks before adding them to a dish.

To obtain their full flavour, fresh herbs must be bruised or chopped in order to release the aromatic oils. So, even if you are putting some thyme, parsley and bay in a simple bouquet garni, crush the leaves gently to release the flavours.

When cooking with dried herbs, extra flavour can be extracted from them before they are added to a dish by warming the herb gently, either spread out on a baking sheet in a very low oven, or in a dry frying pan (skillet) over a very low heat for 3–4 minutes, until fragrant.

Herbs are generally added towards the end of a dish's cooking time to preserve their flavour.

PREPARING IN ADVANCE

It is always a good plan to prepare the main dishes of any Indian meal in advance. The flavours and spices will then have time to realize their true potential. Make the dish and leave it overnight or for up to 3 days in the refrigerator, before being reheated and served. Freezing the cooked dish will have the same effect.

Preparing the dish in advance will allow you extra time to put together the other essential components of the meal and to concentrate on the presentation of the dishes, which adds to the complete Indian gastronomic experience – presentation is never a last-minute thought in an Indian household, but an integral part of the meal.

Fresh Seasoning Mix

This is a fresh seasoning mix that is a personal favourite. It can be added to any of the recipes in this book – add it at the end to give the dish a sharp edge.

2 tbsp coriander (cilantro) leaves and stalks, chopped finely
1 tbsp lime juice
1 green chilli, deseeded and chopped finely

1. Mix all the ingredients together just before using.

INDEX